Of Granddaughters and Mars

Also by Donald Mace Williams

Wolfe and Being Ninety

The Nectar Dancer

Poems by Rainer Maria Rilke: A 150th Anniversary Reader

Beowulf: For Fireside and Schoolroom

Timberline, U.S.A.

Interlude in Umbarger

Of Granddaughters and Mars

Poems by

Donald Mace Williams

Paperback: 978-1-965766-83-5
Ebook: 978-1-965766-84-2
Library of Congress: 2026906087

Cover photo by Gael Cunningham. Cover concept by John Wilson.
Author photo by Dagmar Grieder

Printed in the United States

Contents

Calls for Help

Mars: A Quartet

Still Here

For My Granddaughters' Birthdays

Reconstructions

Unfettered Breezes

Neo-Saxonians

Zebulon

German Romantic Poets

Aboard an Austrian Train at Ninety-Four

This is my first and surely last trip here.
The train slips eastward in Tyrolean silence
across the sweet toes of the poets' Alps,
whose ranks once would have made my rib cage lift
in Keatsian surmise, as if this range
still had one unclimbed, unromanticized
summit or knife-edge. Yesterday I rode
three cable cars up to the scabs of snow
on a bare field that in my former Rockies
would surely have shown whortleberries, grass,
and yipping pikas. Or am I inventing,
remembering former remembering?
My unused memories are scarce these days.

How many miles ago was my first love,
which like a mountain range drew me across
sharp ridges, down scree slopes, into
new explorations, new bewilderments?
Twelve thousand miles a year times seventy,
all of them whispers now like this slick train.

We've come past Würgl, a village whose name
sounds like overindulgence but whose scenes
in this late summer are all peptic green,
cows lying in a pastoral repose
though some of the pastures are steep enough to be
ibex golf courses. All of them are mown,
I think, by elf greenskeepers in the night.
So this is love, too, and is truth, this beauty

that slithers by as fast as if my miles
remaining had become kilometers.
I won't try changing their allegro back
to moderato. What I pass, let pass.
I tilt my seat back like a sloping field
and lie sustained and eased by so much green.

Calls for Help

1. The Need of More Navalnys

He went foreknowingly homeward to death—
before home, almost, poison-scourged en route.
His cross was prison, each day a new nail,
chosen and suffered in his hope to save
Russians from Russians. May it be so, and may
some new Navalny, now, save us from us,
or manifold Navalnys, living still,
do so by word and act, by sacrifice,
speaking for us in shackled eloquence
in their name and all patriots' names, and God's.

2. A Modern Monster

December, 2024

In high school, dear old Mrs. Skidmore taught
us *Beowulf*, including lines in our
long vanished language, sounds of strange, dark power,
which, although badly mispronounced, still caught
my ear and mind to stay, till finally I
left city desk and typewriter to do
years of new studies and at length grind through
my own translation, all to find out why
that long and brutal poem, through grim years
of wars, uprisings, and elections, still
rings out like chain mail in our cybered ears.
The answer looms now. From his joyless lair
across dank moors, his teeth bared for the kill,
stalking, comes Grendel. Beowulf, help!--if you dare.

3. Of Angels Bending Near the Earth to Touch Their Harps of Gold

At ten, I thought they really touched their harps
onto the ground, to charge ethereal gold
with earthly pulses and to give us then
their own chords, full of heaven-help for us.
What I imagine now is that when they
are home again, they strum out all they learned
in their reconnaissance: much motion here,
the mini-imps jab-jabbing upward through
our surface tension like hell-sent cicadas
to scream our lynchings at us, our gulags,
enslavings, burnings at the stake, and wars,
and, done with those, the final horror, soon,
the sacrifice of love to mere know-how.
Come down again now, angels, take and give,
before we end God's--who knows, trillionth?--try
for some Earth not inventing its own death.

Maria's Rescue

Before this, she had shown us she was brave,
Opposing him, which meant an outlawed life,
But now it must have seemed that each great wave
Had been Maduro-raised, a hovering knife.

Battered and soaked, she with the gallant crew
Survived, an in absentia laureate
Who with God's help will guide her country through
A tyrant sea to where free ways await.

A Ghazal on the Threat of War

If we should lift the bar once more
That opens onto war once more,

If we should join the ravaged world
In war that starts afar once more

And does not stay but strikes this house
Or here, now, blasts this car: Once more

Men, women, children fall and die
As some wild, worshipped tsar once more

Or home-grown tyrant shows his power
And our worst weres are ares once more.

Mars: A Quartet

1. After Landing

I take a minute to consider where
I stand. Of course outside the vehicle,
on hard red soil, but otherwise: without
communication, power, any chance
of rescue, not before my food supply
gives out, and water, too, unless the hike
I'm almost set to start on shows there is
a spring here, potable of course, because
what, here, could taint it, or the air, if there
were air? This is pure solitude at last,
unbounded and for now at least unthreatened.
I stretch with pleasure and begin my walk.
Bow low, red nothing, your king has arrived.

2. To a Red-Soil Microbe

Small thing to carry such a load
(they do say you had DNA),
did your descendant, down that road
three billion drawn-out years away,

set out for some Olympus Mons
of deathlessness and, swathed and masked
in technics, shunning pros and cons,
find final answers, all unasked?

(Volcanic whimsy, don't you know?)
Or just as likely, you were it,
the start and end, the whole brief show,
an undivided micro-bit.

No lesson for us then, in how
one scene leads to a trillion scenes,
all saying to our deepened brow,
you can't escape, it's in the genes.

3. Capsuled Home

For all that time, I was device,
only as part of science real,
recording airless atmosphere,
treading on dirt I could not feel.

Down now, I gorge on ambient air
and stamp on real turf, joyfully.
Still, inside, science looms. I strip,
outsprint pursuit. I climb a tree.

4. A Martian Dig

Its kind now having neutralized all life
on Earth, an astrorobot, newly come,
is bent on seeing if this bare, red planet
holds any hint of former flesh-and-blood
inhabitants. It digitally digs,
a sensor for its spade, and what is this?
"Astonishment and thrill," it registers.
Deep down the time-tiers of this empty land
is the clear imprint of a robot's foot.

Still Here

A Flood

We never heard it coming, never saw or felt it,
but woke up with it everywhere, inside, outside.
No point getting on the roof, there was no top
or bottom to this, no dimension, only presence,
made known as total, instant, flooding numbness. What
was there before last night? Have we lost all of it?
Now this is all of it. How did we get along
before the thick tree trunks of what we thought was thought
became these splintered stems, around which, every day,
the newness slaloms silently, bringing our lunch?

2084

Life used to be. Back then we thought its end
mighty and dreadful, which was so, and so
life stayed the more alive, however short.
Peaks, true, there were, and pits, and light and gloom,
and knowledge that their ends were soon to come
kept love alive, and love kept life alive.
Now no one dies, or loves. Life, you are dead.

Mozart's Piano

Surely there slumbers, deep in wood,
a shred of sound his fingers struck.
Start cloning, science, hide for good
other pursuits in compu-muck.

I don't want AI's summoned psalms
on depths its icy brain has plumbed,
but revenant music: Handel, Brahms,
what tunes the Lascaux painters hummed.

From an Airplane at Night

There, miles across anonymous city lights
a flicker comes, one only, salient,
bright and then quickly gone again. In Maine,
from dockside when the bay was ceilinged by
gray-massed, schooled herring, countless, hovering
acres of tail and scale, and as the day
began to dim, I saw one silver flash,
too brief to time, from one fish, only one,
and then gray, darker than before. Mozart,
I think, and Keats. How to account for flashes?

Austin in August

Juniper hills have replaced rock ledges with code-gated houses.
Million-dollar live oaks' limbs hang frozen mid-writhe.
Downtown, competitive towers keep lights on in empty windows.
Eastward are small wooden houses with part-time taquerias.
The broad granite Capitol reddens the scene, evoking the past.
Scooter riders slip along First like conveyor-belt statues.
Homeless people's cardboard signs spell most things right.
Tattooed women pushing strollers wait for the walk lights.
The iron hand rail is too hot to touch. Will October come?

Guadalupe

Rain had long been desired, but when the owls,
Awake in scrub-oaks on the steep, dark hills,
Saw what was taking form a long way down,
They quavered out their wonder, predators
Astounded at the size of that brown hunter
Surging with open mouth, omnivorous,
Swallowing flesh as heedlessly as wood
And fur (of the stuffed bears it tore away
From small girls'grasps, then taking, too, the girls)
And, after full daylight came, sinking back,
Sated, to its old silence, as the owls
Shuffled the rain off their brown wings and slept.

Autumnal Falls

Now, on my front lawn, red,
gold, amber, leaves lie spread,
their spines and vee-shaped veins
brought out by this week's rains,
gently discarded things,
like fairies' molted wings.

Rainbow, Garden of the Gods

Done with the day's work,
The gardeners troop homeward
Along the cool bridge.

Brought Back

Scientists hope to restore
the mammoth herds.

I hate this place. How can I get away?
None of my friends are here, none of the herd.
Back where I was, I knew them, every one,
their smells, their sounds, the tapers of their tusks.
Just strangers here. Strange to each other, too.
Where did they come from? Where did I? I fell,
I know that, through the ice, into the stream,
too careless. Then I was a calf again,
now this. It's hot here, the snow underfoot
practically sweats, and when that's pawed, the ground
gives out almost a tepid breath. The grass
is lush, all right, but watery, insipid.
The birches grow too tall, too thick. The bark
is juiceless. Everything is easy. Food,
such as it is, comes also on the backs
of those fast pests that roar along and clank
and have their bellies full of creatures like
men, somewhat, although pale and nearly hairless.
I hate those things, and just the other day
enjoyed the privilege of knocking one
flat on its side with one swipe of a tusk.
It lay there with its legs in a wild whirl
till others drove me back, a pack like wolves.
I blame them all for doing this to me.
Somehow they brought me to this gutless place
where bears have short claws and long noses, where
elk run away, not staring straight ahead,
antlers like landscapes, daring you to fight.
Peace is the way here. Fighting is passé.

I tried, when flat-head, there, was moving in
on her, the one whose season was upon her.
I took three steps, snorted, pawed snow, and boom!
From nowhere, two of those weird things roared up
and blocked my way. What business do they have
telling us whom to couple with? I want
to go home, fight and mate, be on my guard
against that motley, vicious, splendid horde
of enemies with fangs and spears, that want
me dead. I want to smell my neighbors' sweat,
eat pungent sedges, scrape at honest ice.
I loved that place, my home. Where has it gone?

Approaching Herd

Painting by Frank Reaugh, in the Panhandle-Plains Historical Museum, Canyon, Texas

They have come over the rise, these fifteen Longhorns,
And the heads and horns of more are just behind.
Of the front bunch, the pale one with high head,
Alert and even speculative, and
Delicate in spite of weighing, surely,
A ton, has horns swept up like wondering eyebrows:
"Why is that gray-haired cowboy sitting there
On a small, cross-leggèd wooden horse
And holding, not reins, but a bristly stick
And staring at me as if looking for
A difference from all the other steers?"
The others plod with cumbersome heads down,
Hoping, if they hope anything, the man
Doesn't intend to brand them with that stick
As if they had turned into calves again.
No barbed-wire fences show behind the herd,
But nearby those grow exponentially.

The Longhorns' time is almost finished, since
Postholes are sinking and house-skeletons
Rising, unseen as yet by them. Today,
Beneath jet trails, captive and on display,
Three remnant ruminants with horns as wide
As flatbeds chew hay in their little pen,
Thinking of nothing more than food, if that,
Not noticing the picture-taking tourists.

A Faceless Air

Love

When love was still some years ahead,
I knew very well how it would be.
On a dewy morning, I and she
would stroll out in the April red:
We shall turn to see, in the silvered field,
The green where we have walked,
And light as dewdrops on the grass
You will lay your hand upon my arm.
She, the real she, and I, by then
as real as I would ever get,
walked on brown grass no dew had wet.
A kingbird perched, flew, perched again
along the barbed wire, on and on,
always a few fenceposts ahead.
Fly to the side, dummy, she said.
We laughed. Ah, where have those days gone?

The Circle

The plains rise a little from here, and three miles or more
away, they stop, it seems to my eye. If I
were a compass and my long arm turned the horizon,
the edges of the bowl I'm in, my chalk would score
more finitely yet the circumference of my seeing.
Except that far beyond that, high and small,
geese form a line as if scored by a hand and arm.
Don't radii have to cease where the circle ceases?
I thought they did, before, but this new concept,
released from mere landlocked geometry,
draws my eyes upward from the rim of ranchland.
Wonderful geese, float high and far beyond me,
tell me her life wasn't after all circumscribed
by the ring that closed around it when she died.

Extrapolating from the World

I take it God approves of wars
and death and such,
but clearly also birds and flowers
and a lover's touch.

It may be bipolarity
or some worse illness
or else, in words I dislike to see,
mere stillness.

A Ghazal on Time

"Is there time?"
"Define time."

"Time eats life,
Life eats time,

Mealtime done,
No more time."

"Still, though God
Knows no time,

When we pray,
It's for time."

Facing Pages

There isn't anyone I'd rather grow old with,
she said, and I said the same, and we grew old.
And one of us died, and there isn't anyone
whose voice I'd rather hear, whose small hand hold.

We sat together and read, and I made sounds,
not words, acknowledging our closeness. No,
our close apartness, as on facing pages.
The pages will meet, the book close, when I go.

Unbraced

I stepped into a cold, clear morning
and thought at first there was no breeze.
To make sure, I stood still, and, ah,
the day moved toward me faintly, all
the air together, with no sound
of breath, a faceless air, not pursed
as if to kiss or swaddling me
like breezes of the long, long day
before, scarcely a breeze at all.
Surely, deprived of anything
to open to, my arms would wither,
my unbraced knees would buckle. Now
I see how stark such stillness is,
how close to death. Stir stronger, love.

To a Fashion School Graduate

For Miranda

What sentient people choose to wear
On what occasion, when and where,
Is one expression of the quest
For beauty, which, as Keats said best,
Is truth. So truth is your career,
Or soon will be, and when you hear
The words and tones that mean delight
In what you've done, may that sweet night
Make worthwhile those years of your youth
Learning the wardrobe ways of truth.

To Dagmar

2022

Dasha, you've seen the world so much
And filled shelves with the evidence--
With objets d'art I don't dare touch,
Brought home by you, the Lord knows whence--

That if I joined them up there
As if, like them, to be with you,
I'd flown by maybe Swazi Air,
And learned their tongues, all forty-two,

I still would feel so out of place,
So hickish, so afraid to frown
Lest I dislodge some ancient vase,
I would want only one thing: down.

Then, by your side, sweet worldly one,
I would not think of mosque or dome
But only of contentment, won
From you, who are my longed-for home.

For My Granddaughters' Birthdays

(Back Then)

III

I held you upside down
Where the ocean rolled in thin,
And you reached to feel the water
Cool on your skin.

Your aunt said, "Taste your finger."
You did, then held it for me
While the little waves kept toppling
As white as could be.

The taste of seashore salt
Is full of wind and ships.
Its smell is in the air,
Its feel is on your lips.

I hope that sea-salt taste
Stays with you all your years
And never, never mingles
With the taste of tears.

V

I hear you're good at chess.
I'm quite a player, too.
I either know or guess
What all the pieces do.

Well, maybe not. One thing
I do know is the men,
Like there's a bean, a wing,
Books, yawns, hiccups, and then—

What are those other pieces?
Someone turn up the lights.
I see now, they're gray geeses.
Not right? OK, they're bites.

So yawns, on top, are round,
Books look like little castles,
The wing and bean are crowned,
Hiccups have caps, not tassels.

But what about those others?
Why, bites have horses' heads.
They're sisters, or else brothers.
They spend their nights in sheds.

I saw a set so tall
The moves were made with pickups—
Yawns, books, beans, wings, and all,
Great bites, and monstrous hiccups.

VII

Since I speak only English
And just a little Morse,
It makes me feel all tinglish
When you converse in Horse.

To learn Chinese or Greek
Is hard enough, and so
Just how you learn to speak
In Horse, I'd like to know.

Next time you're coming here,
Study your Granddadese
So you can make that clear.
You will come, won't you? Please?

IX

You know how, every school-day morning,
Out the front door and to your right,
As long as it's not wet or cloudy,
Down Silverwood the sun's in sight.

I wonder, now, how it would be
If, all your getting-ready done,
You stepped outside and, hey, what's this?
There, on your *left*, arose the sun.

"Daddy, what's going on?" you'd say,
And he would stare and rub his eyes
And go inside to see if Mommy,
Like him, had mixed up set with rise.

But no. The westward sun kept climbing
And soon the street was full of neighbors
All buzzing, gesturing, or praying,
And none gone off to books or labors.

OK, you might decide, so east
Just didn't have its hooks in dawn
As deeply as we thought. Now west
Becomes the place days start out on.

Tell me, though, would it be so simple?
What changes would we have to learn?
And what reversal caused it all?
I'll let you say. It's your, uh, turn.

IX-2

When you sit down to play a scale,
Each finger to its own white key,
It goes like this, in keyboard Braille:
C D E F G A B … *¿sí?*

Bueno. But now there comes in sight
A note marked *b* or #. With that,
One finger rises left or right
To play a black note, sharp or flat.

A note like that, an "accidental,"
Not part of what the scale expects,
Gives pleasure, audial and mental—
Or else it runs off course and wrecks.

If well-used, though, it gives a tune
A sweet twist for a while, and then
Not too much later or too soon
The note drops out. You're home again.

("Home" is the scale you first had played.)
And yet, it isn't quite the same.
The detour and return you made
Have changed its mood, if not its name.

Haven't you, too, made some small change
Of ways, changed back within the day,
And felt at home, but one shade strange?
People and music grow that way.

X

At night in the lit-up city sky
Stars are pale and far between.
Now, three in the morning, summer, no moon,
Dark in the mountains like farm-child nights,
The Milky Way is as white
As a row of cotton on deep black land,
Ready for picking. You grasp and pull
Star after star, each from its boll,
A Velcro sound. Into the bag
On your shoulder they go.
Then you gin, and mill, and spin, and weave,
And make a dress that's bright as gold—
But only when it's worn at night
A long way from a clashing light.

X-2

I'm not quite sure what part of you
Gave rise to that bright, instant glow
When you met Sarah, but I, too,
Must have lit up, it pleased me so.

So this, I thought, is what is needed
To bring such joy to that sweet face
When nothing else has quite succeeded:
This smaller child to hug and chase.

Was it a child's delight in play
Or a soft surge of woman-to-be
That brought about that warm display?
(Either, or both, was fine with me.)

XI

When I was a kid, the countryside
I read about was far away—
In England, say, or Tennessee—
And nothing Texan had a say.

So scrub oaks, phlox, and prickly pear,
I thought, weren't worth the written word,
Without which, I gave second place
To things I only saw or heard.

Since then, I've come to see two things:
The land I live in *is* in books,
And anyway, my own eyes count—
No need to read how something looks.

Now, this is in no way to say
We don't need books. You and I do,
For sure. But they're not everything,
And print's not all that makes truths true.

So let's try, you and me, to look
At things and people with clear eyes
So if some book says they're worthwhile,
"Do tell!" we'll say. "Surprise, surprise!"

Reconstructions

I. Vaughan Williams:

Fantasia on a Theme of Thomas Tallis

It moves through columned mysteries,
This holy essence, veiled by scrims
Of mist in bronze interstices
Where sunrise strikes the high, arched beams.

We cannot tell whether with voice
Or impulse only this procession
Swells the dim air: it is a place
Where voice and thought make no distinction.

Nor is it certain whether woods
Of ivied oak or some great church
Is host to what comes by--this flood
Of awe, this ghostly, primal march.

It passes; then, amassed once more,
Rises, surrounds us with ourselves
Before it ends: all that we are,
Nothing we know. Our souls, our cells.

II. Ravel:

String Quartet in F

The open walls let evening air
into the dance
and she is the dance.

The outburst isn't thunder
but she, demanding
why, tenacious, intense.

Music, amnesiac, again,
but the past pulsing
beneath. All he will say

is because. And the dance now
wilder, too crazy
for Q and A.

One immerses oneself
in flingings, grimaces.
But ah (outside now), *¿porqué*?

A night bird, the moon,
whispers, then silence,
a look, an uncertain kiss.

Daytime: machines, and he,
watchful, between. The dance
pounds; steel arms hook and release.

III. Brahms:

Piano Concerto No. 2

The dining hall is full of brown, warm light,
The table weighted down with old-style dishes--
Roast beef with browned potatoes, yeasty breads--
The diners in coats, vests, ties, long gowns, amber
Curved combs in thick, upswept, honey-hued hair,
Using last names--"Miss," "Mister"--all but speaking
In meter, putting the occasional popular phrase
In vocal quotes. An oak fire warms the back
Of the host to this manorial meal, who carves,
Passing down loaded plates and morsels of wit.
Dated, perhaps, and stiff, but in a glow
You soon see comes from restless minds, too keen
To let the postures of their time restrict
Their outreach, and broad souls, warmed by a matchless
Claret, ennobling food and talk. At first
The men are dominant, affairs of state,
Hunting, and dogs their substance. Such insights,
Such stories, genial, never malicious,
You do not hear these days, much less such voices.
After a silence during which the faces
Lighten, redden a bit from the great wine,
A new turn on the same ideas comes,
A vibrant, teasing, questioning response
From women, caught up here, then here, till all
The company seems bright with joy, the host
Smiling, the fireplace filled with airy flame.
Surprising, then, after that cordial uproar
Subsides, to have one voice emerge, a woman's,
And strike a note of melancholy, of loss.
She speaks so raptly it is as if she

Were all her audience, and so lyrically,
A celebration of sorrow, that all hushes
And no one moves as long as she is speaking.
But this mood, sad and lovely, can not last
Amid such company, such food. She stops,
And soon a burst of cheer and optimism
Resounds, the table almost whirls, the guests,
Even the pensive one of moments ago,
Buoyed up by pleasure. So the dinner ends
With coffee, pudding, pulling back of chairs,
Quick bows, and, suddenly, as if this great
Bodily warmth and brilliance, the joy and wit,
The momentary sadness, even the food,
So rich and filling, had been after all
A feast of spirits or gods, the guests dissolve,
Vanish. The table shines, fresh-laid, and only
The outlines of the guests hang in the air
Like images of light on closed eyelids
Or French-horn resonances living on
In polished walls after a concert ends.

Unfettered Breezes

Six Bugologues

1. Black Widow

When I first saw you, I thought yes,
you're what I've always hoped to meet,
your roundness, sleekness, glossiness,
that hourglass figure, red and sweet,
on your beneath, such genteel spines
on your hind legs, and such cute fangs.
Come closer now, my heart repines
for your dear self. My future hangs
on your consent. No question: I,
to have your love, would gladly die.

2. Praying Mantis

Like twigs-and-stem I lie by day
and, elbows under chin, await
whatever bugs are sent my way—
by heaven, you know, not merely fate.

If, say, a cricket happens by
and lights a little farther out
on this, my weed, I won't ask why.
It came because I've been devout.

And so I eat it, prayerfully,
this leg, then that, and now the head,
crunchy and warm, while juice runs free.
That's how it comes, my daily bread.

3. Cicada

For endless years in bug gulag,
I lived dark-swaddled, lived to grope
through hairlike curtains of root-clog—
withheld from liberty, not hope.

Now, having burst up through earth's crust
to where unfettered breezes blow,
I sing, of course, my pent-up lust,
but freedom, too, fortissimo.

4. gnat

my role is small, a dot with wings,
but all of us must act our part
as if it were the lead. mine brings
applause that's clearly from the heart.

it may seem strange, perhaps unfair,
that my part's always such a hit
when staged on nothing but warm air,
but so it is when on i flit.

i know the people love my work
because they clap so furiously,
right in my face. they go berserk.
an encore, then, or two, or three.

5. Fly

I'm of a most distinguished line.
It springs from one poetic hero
whose fame can never see decline
till brains (like, sometimes, bones) read zero.

The generations since his time
number two thousand, more or less,
a month each, and through all, the rhyme
has sung my forebear's worthiness.

My many-times-great-granddad's breath
breathes on—a sound that truly was
heard at a poet's fancied death:
a famous fly's immortal buzz.

6. Cockroach

I had bad dreams all night, and when
I woke up, found myself transformed
Into a monstrous thing, with chin
And teeth, two leggèd and two armed.

What's this, I asked myself, a dream?
No dream. I lay and tried to think.
All was familiar. But the seam
I slept in, underneath the sink,

Was far too narrow for me now.
How could I wriggle out? At last,
Contorting and in pain, somehow
I managed. But, that trial passed,

I had to move, to feed and forage
As always, and what would they say,
My friends, the bugs? I summoned courage
And set out on my upright way.

Five Bird Words

1. Cardinal

Last year, when I was young, I heard
On all sides TEE-oo Whit-Whit-Whit,
Full voiced, most beautiful, but now
Two trees from mine, some yearling twit
Stutters out TYOO-ch-ch-ch-ch
And other trees for miles around
Echo that senseless, tuneless sound,
New-style. Alas for lass and lad,
Love songs aren't sung this spring but chirred,
And if some kid says, "Like that, Dad?"
I'll have to tell him, "Not one Whit."

2. Mourning Dove

I love mild summer evenings and cool dawns.
Those, and not grief, draw gentle tones from me.
Let them declare me mournful if they will,
My song floats cloudlike outward from the tree
And soothes the pasture in damp mystery.

3. Mockingbird

A glorious morning, and delightful, too,
Some lucky lady in some blessed tree,
Freedom, freedom, oh callay, calloo,
Look at me jumping, looklooklooka me.
Graack graack graack graack a stately pleasure dome,
A book of verses drop drop dead drop dead,
Tee-oo whit whit show me the way to go home.
And spend spend spend the rest of my life in bed.
A tune hangs seconds in my head, in vain
I try to shake it, shake I say, shake shake,
But mousie, mousie, thou art no thy lane
Come, sweet bird lady, come and no mistake.
I wait, I flag, I sing spring sing spring sing,
And we will all the pleasures prove. Spring! Spring!

4. Chickadee

I'm perky and small, I sing dee-dee-dee,
My flock is one pulsing, flittery thing,
Within which it makes no difference to me
Whether upright I perch or upside-down cling.

If you see a small tree seem to shake on its own
As if all of its leaves were astir in a breeze
Though the air is dead-calm, we've made ourselves known,
The bringers of warm, feathered motion to trees.

5. Peacock

That's mine, the magnificent tail
I hoist like a gaudy sail.
It's huge, with a hundred eyes.
It's raised with intent to surprise
And charm the admiring claques
Of peahens. All that lacks
In my charm arsenal
Is what serves to woo and lull:
Sweet song. I practice, though.
Listen now, here I go.
Met-filling high notes, true?
What's that? Met-emptying, too?
All right, but now watch this.
Spread, tail! See? It can't miss.

Neo-Saxonians

In the style of Anglo-Saxon riddles

Changeable Presence

Shaper and batterer, soother of victims,
Now low, now high lingering, dashing,
Blue-skinned or green, or brown, whitely crowned,
Servant and poisoner, poised to arise
In life and beauty when bonds hold her,
Death and suffering when sundered from those.
Her soft body is sought by men
Both night and day, but death visits,
With writhing and fear, those who find her unsought.
And while one grows weary, wishing her elsewhere,
Another's chants fill chapels with pleas
That her gentle touch, tiresome before,
Come, night or noon, and nevermore leave.

The Domestication

With huffings and blats they hied themselves
Into our presence, eagerly massed,
Warm though weightless, awaiting their call
And the wished-for burdens that a breath would load
Or a sob, a shudder, a seething rage.
In time, conceiving, we took them on,
Fumblingly first then faster, learning,
Our skill as packers improving till
In a single moment we could send hundreds
Abroad, laden with burdens of ours
Though they, unseen, lacked substance and bone.
This, too, we found: these flying things,
Energized air, once out, were gone.
No tears of ours could toll them back.
The wonder is how, once, as they milled,
Their strength unguessed, we stood unbroken
By loads that the moaning herds longed to take from us.

Sweet and Sour

One door of five welcomes this guest.
Though bringing burdens she bears ours away.
Two staffs support her when, skipping, hobbling,
In black-dotted dress she dances by;
Warmly invited, once taken in
Hard to send home, she heals with charm
But her darker side saddens us too.
Let a scene be merry, she makes it so,
Yet some in her nearness never feel joy.
Quarreled over, misunderstood,
She speaks a language souls only know.

Low-Born Emperor

Lacking in weight, he wields masses,
Their roar and flash, fury and drive,
And seething casters of cargoes of fire
Arcwise across the emptied land.
Those ragings tethered, he takes the field
In cleats and helm, or counts his triumphs
Where charts tally, or chattering drills,
Inroads on enemies. But this awesome force
With the toothy, stuttering stich-halving name
Is blind and deaf, bodiless, silent,
Abiding in murk, elemental, unseen,
Driving half the world with his heedless stir,
An arch power spawned in a seedy room.

Defier of Gravity

Up is his down, his easy path,
Down his downfall. Death can win him
Through his own gorging, this guest's custom
When all unbidden he breezes in
And loud, arrogant, eats poor wretches
Out of house and home. But heaped tables,
Meats in abundance, manage no more
To ease his hunger than empty ones,
And dinner over he dies on the spot,
Or unappeased prowls to the neighbors',
Merry fellow, for more glutting,
Then, dead or alive, leaves his hosts
In the black, bankrupt, brief though his stay was,
A monster, clearly, missed by no one,
His rude arrival rued and lamented.
How different, though, when, duly met,
Calm and engaging, he graces a room,
The loved center of circled talk,
Fed, though not petted, a peerless uniter.
At length, when left, he lingers all night,
Dying, paling, till people stir
And a breathed greeting brings back his smile.

Continuous Gestation

Winking, wobbling, a womb with eyes,
Fertile as catfish, fleet and languid,
Her Weltanschauung voluble, silent,
Arachnidlike, her legsprawl flattened,
She waits for her partner: approach, embrace,
A fecund exchange, and she's full again,
Always pregnant, her inside bumped
By heads and elbows till the hour arrives,
Months in the making, of her motherhood.
Delivery done, no lag granted,
In her round belly brood stirs anew,
Her hands-off doctors heard but not seen,
Her days a rush, her regimen endless.

Skyline Herds

On the high mesa where mustangs posed,
New presences playing, feeding:
Lipizzaners, long-backed and elegant,
Rearing whitely, radiant hooved,
Princely bodies pawing in unison
As if sky were soil and snow covered
Their airy fodder, Aeolian hay.
Fruitful their scraping for such herds now
Mount the skylines of many a range,
Proliferant, pale, looming and grand,
Wayland's remudas windily pastured.

Change of Pace

Sluggard and lingerer he lagged to the rear,
Heedless of pleas, of my hands' exhorting,
My poundwood tantrums, torpor, anguish
At stone-booted slouchiness, spite, mockery.
Then how does it happen with hateful speed
Silent footed he flits ahead
While leadshod I lumber, logy and tired,
Wasted, my calls to wait, to tarry,
My eyes, astrain, seeking him out,
Distant and dwindling, when, decades past,
No fury of mine could move him to hasten?

Ceaseless Laborer

Soother, subverter, vein opener,
Crasher of barricades, comforter of pain,
Limitless ranging, lightlike my speed,
My intimates countless, confidants few,
By dark or day dealing alike
With hermits and hosts, unhurried, sure,
Manifold-featured, now masked, now flensed,
Or vague, whispering, I visit all
Whether late or soon, longed-for or fled,
With never a pause in my peregrination
Nor weariness, nor wishing myself
Applause, welcome, wealth or comfort.
As for security, who claims as much?
I need only number my deeds
So as not to see, some smoke-red dawn,
I have done so well no work survives.

Youth and Age

Playful in childhood, prancingly bright,
Heels high-kicking in heedless joy,
He shuns profundity, freedom his creed,
Treble his tunings, untroubled songs.
One day he wakens to deeper tones
And slow awarenesses, solemn reflections.
Darker his way now, winsomeness past,
Burdens abounding, by breadth supported
And helpers' backs. Happy no more,
He labors darkly, at last coming
Gloomy and old to the end decreed,
His tongue tasting tears for his youth.

Zebulon

“Discoverer” of Pikes Peak

I.

It must have been hell, serving under him,
Scrubbing pots in the night to the howls of wolves
While he sat on a log by the fire and scribbled,
Or trenching his tent with red hands in a marsh
Frozen so hard the shovel made no more
Of a dent in it than teeth in the leg of the old
Grouse cock that he or Miller shot one day
Out hunting with that lady rifle of his.
He made them all jump overboard to drag
The expedition's boats over icy rocks.
While he wrote he looked up now and then
With his head cocked to the right, the way he did
When he ordered a hundred lashes for the man
Who on the Mississippi let the flag
Be stolen from the boat at night, except
Now he was only mumbling words to himself,
Sometimes in French, before he put them down.
The kind of officer his soldiers hated, you'd think,
Especially those, like most of the twenty or so
On either of his expeditions, who couldn't
So much as sign their names. Hate him? The way
Enlisted men always hate officers,
Yes, and slaves masters, peasants feudal lords:
Obligatory hate, impersonal scowls.
Still, nearly all who took that first cruel trip
Up the Mississippi to what young Pike
Thought was its source, went also on the second,
Crueler yet—frost maiming the ragged men—
And by their own choice. One thing, Pike pitched in,
Breaking trail for Miller in the deep snow

All the way to the lake Pike wrongly thought
Was what he wrongly thought he had been sent
To find: the white womb and icy cervix where
The river of his trials squirmed into its own.
This making the source of the river the sine qua non
Of his exploring, though his orders put
Finding sites for forts and calming the tribes
Above it, shows Pike a bad interpreter
Of orders, as he was of men and mountains
And lakes and, last, of ammunition dumps.
Or does it, like his greenhorn straying, later,
Toward the Great Peak he never set a foot on
(Though his name took root up there so early
That time wore off its very apostrophe)
Show something in him that his shavetail airs
Never suggested? Sources, pinnacles:
They were the sirens, loreleis, belles dames
Who mercilessly drew Pike on and up,
Then let him live. Zebulon Pike had a vision
Always before him, though usually blurred.

"Zebulon:" no. He never went by that
But always by his middle name, Montgomery,
Though he signed orders Z.M., and self-justifying
Letters to that arch scoundrel whom he worshiped,
The thieving double-crosser Wilkinson,
General and traitor, whose majestic purity Pike
No more questioned than that of the Great Peak
He calculated was eighteen thousand five hundred
And some odd feet above sea level—only
Forty-four hundred feet too high. But that
Came on the second trip, the western one.
Wilkinson sent him first not over mountains
But up a river, *the* river, in eighteen-five.
This was new land, still called Louisiana.

The nation needed word of how it lay.
"You will be pleased to take the course of the River,"
Wilkinson said, and specified the details
He should note down, among them prairies, islands,
Shoals, rapids, timber, Indian villages,
Weather and wind, how many animal skins
Indians bartered and for what return,
From whom, and where they mostly did their hunting.
Find sites for two new military posts,
Said Wilkinson, and get the Indians' consent,
"Informing them that they are intended to increase
Their trade" and otherwise improve their lot.
"You will proceed," the order said, "to ascend
The main branch of the River, until you reach
The source of it." But, Wilkinson went on,
He should go that far only if in no danger
Of being caught by freezeup before he returned.
What did Pike do? He pushed up toward the source,
Sure that to find it was worth frostbite, hunger,
And disregarding orders, that ambition
And curiosity outweighed all else,
As if the only reasonable end
To a trip upriver was the starting place of the river
And turning back with that unfound was treason,
If not to his country, to one Lieutenant Pike.

They set out from St. Louis, that August day,
With kegs of whisky for trading and morale
On board the boats, and also violins,
Which the soldier explorers played one day
In mid-September when the sailing was fair.
A month past that, they waded up to their necks
Four hours, Pike, really, in there along with his men,
Dragging their boats upstream, snow falling, till all became
"Perfectly useless in our limb's with cold"

And went ashore to build a fire. There they discovered
Leaks in both boats, and Sergeant Kennerman,
"One of the stoutest men I ever knew,"
Pike said, threw up two quarts of blood from bailing.
Feeling pity then "for those poor fellows
Who, to obey my orders were killing themselves,"
Pike ordered all back to camp to fell pine trees
And make canoes, a few days' work. Those done,
They loaded one with goods and ammunition.
It promptly sank, and Pike put his soaked gunpowder
In pots by the fire to dry like cookie dough
Or, as it happened, like a kid who puts
Firecrackers in a tin can for the boom.
The explosion must have frightened bears and foxes
For miles around. So that was one more thing
Pike wasn't good at judging. No one died,
But the event foresaw the rest of the trip,
A tale of men and sleds falling through ice,
Of scouting parties lost for days, of Pike
And other men caught out on hunting trips
And sleeping blanketless in snow, of cold
So hard that fingers, toes, and noses froze
Like garden hoses on cold nights. "My boys,"
Pike called his men, or "my lads," or, in the case
Of his young orderly, "my little boy,"
But later, in a letter, they were "dam'd rascels"—
No conflict there, to parents of small boys,
But what he meant was their unletteredness,
Their chewing with open mouths, their filthy words,
Their love of booze, no doubt their bedding of squaws,
Whereas he claimed in his journals to have
Turned down the offer of one of a chief's wives
For a night, explaining what he said was the white man's idea
Of faithfulness. His men must have laughed, though only
Behind hands. This was indeed a rough bunch,

Not much worse off half-barefoot in the snows
Than they would have been "on the outside," at farm
Or factory work back home. But it was more
Than food. They could have stayed on post and slept
Between walls, under roofs. They volunteered
For duty in hell because, hell, nobody else
Had been there. They were like their bookish commander,
Though neither he nor they would like the comparison.
Upstream they wound, as fixedly as if
The source were a magnet towing them by their buckles
As they manned boats, then sleds, then, in deep snow,
Floundered on what they all called rackcts. They lived
On the deer, bear, and elk Pike and two others
Went after day and night. Sometimes there was feasting,
Sometimes two days with nothing in the stomach to build
Warmth in lieu of decent coats and shoes
And to keep strength and spirits up somewhere near
The level of the snow. Louisiana
Back then, now Minnesota: no alligators
But Januarys instead. Pike, on the way,
Had followed orders to the extent of finding
A couple of obvious sites for military posts
And making partial peace between the tribes,
Though knowing it might barely outlast the ice,
And he kept his journal as ordered, though sketchily
And with more to hold readers such as we
Than to help his nation judge how to defend
The new land it had bought. Still, what he wrote,
Evenings, exhausted, his ink freezing, in that
Generic, pompous prose of his, shows him
Moved by the beauty of this unbounded land
As, on the river, the "many beautiful Islands . . .
A prospect so variegated and romantic
That a man may scarcely expect to enjoy such a one
Above twice or thrice in his life." And at the end,

Nearing the climax, to him, of this expedition,
Having fought the snow for miles and left his companion,
The young, strong Miller, behind, he saw a panther,
Twice as big as those downriver, and squatted
In the snow to try to coax it near, the way
We do with a strange, timid dog. No luck,
And probably a good thing for this story,
Because he mightn't have lived to give his name
Unwittingly to that great peak we honor
In honoring Pike and his brave blunderings.
The night of the panther, to Pike and Miller, proved
So cold, some whisky Pike had in a small keg
"Congealed to the consistency of Honey."
Though their blood must have done the same, they left
Their camp early that next day and arrived
At Leech Lake in midafternoon—not much
More detail of this false discovery,
But Pike did note down, "I will not attempt
To describe my feelings on the accomplishment
Of my voyage, this being the main source
Of the Mississippi." How would he feel if he knew
It wasn't the source? But to give him his due,
In that place at that season there was no land,
No lake, no river, anymore than there was birdsong.
Though he mistook this flat white place for the lake
Where it all started, the right flat place wasn't far
To the north, and even when summer brought things out
For what they were, this lake would have looked as likely
As the right one to be the port of departure
Of that sweet cargo of water, soon to darken
With mud and swell and deepen, whose bill of lading
Said "Destination: the Gulf." And having found,
He thought, this starting place, what did he do?
He slogged across the lake, twelve miles, to what
He knew was the Northwest Company's trading post,

And there, with his young companion, was received
"With distinguished politeness and Hospitality"
By one McGillis, a partner in Northwest,
Who served him a late meal of cheese and biscuits,
Coffee and butter—luxuries bespeaking
A way of life well settled on that shore
And in close touch with white men's stores and shippers.
Then how could Pike still claim to be the finder
Of this false source? It must be that Scots traders,
Like Frenchmen, slaves, and Indians, were considered
Unqualified recorders, blind observers
Of starts and middles, ends, and all the moods
Of rapids, copses, marshes, forests, hills
Their moccasins and snowshoes and canoes
Knew to the marrow of each thong and thwart.
True, those were all potential enemies.
For our official and untainted use
Pike brought a useless, wrong, and stale report.
But he brought something else back to Missouri:
A story, words on paper. Whether that
Won wars for us or not, it stocked our cranial
Armories with the fiery shells and bombs
Of the exploring urge. Those helped bring down
A segment of the wall of the unknown,
And institutions grew, for better or worse,
In what we were pleased to call a wilderness.

II.

The Peak stands so far out on the dry plains,
It catches little of the snow that to the west
Smothers the marmots on the Continental Divide
And thaws with a roar into streams, some eastward, some
westward,
That combined would make a dozen Mississippis.
The east side of The Peak, at least, seems more
Like plains exalted than one last great heave
Of eastbound Rockies running out of force.
It sprawls like upward plains and makes no show
Of tall grass or lush flowers, no flute and fiddle
Grace notes and flourishes, only the deep
Warm majesty of cellos and French horns,
But when a tundra wind unfurls a banner
Of horizontal snow out from the top
Like a white warning not to set foot there,
The watchers down on the sunny prairie shiver,
The Peak the tone and temper of their days.
So each day is itself, no light being twice
The same up there in combination with cloud,
Cloud shadows, sky, or teasing girdle of fog
That hides the flanking forests but shows the summit
As red and bare as Mars.
To the flat southeast,
Driving across the sideward plains, you first
See the great peak some miles more west than Pike,
The view made slower now by the floating products
Of affluence and speed. You have passed through
A town with Family Dollar, Duckwall's, and
A red courthouse with jail bars bared out front

Like beavers' teeth. You drive on, peering westward,
Heading up the Arkansas toward Pueblo
As Pike did; and across the rolling brown land
And above the low bluffs to the northwest—is that
Something on the horizon? It's an uplift,
A piece of wall more than a mountain. It shows
Three gables, the one in the middle maybe highest,
But who can measure ghosts? Watching, you drive
Along the road and a web of tracks, both bringing
The east-west trade that's kept the wheatfields green
Most of two centuries, till The Peak has grown
Apart from its companions and above.
But Pike had watched it grow for two slow days
By this stage, and in flatland ignorance
Of western air he thought things were as close
As they seemed to be. He and his men pushed on,
Two days after the sighting, "with an idea
Of arriving at the mountains, but found at night
No visible difference in their appearance," from the day
Before. He had more than The Peak to consider
By now: a party of sixty Pawnees, back
From trying without luck to find some Comanches
To kill, and as Pike knew, such parties, returning,
"Are always ready to embrace an opportunity,
Of gratifying their disappointed vengeance,
On the first persons whom they meet." Pike's party,
Including him, his interpreter, and Robinson,
The doctor, by then had only sixteen, since
Five had set out from the Great Bend of the river
In what became Kansas to float and drag downstream
And note down possibilities and shoals.

Of those remaining in Pike's detachment, twelve,
Three quarters, had been on the Mississippi trip
And, docking in St. Louis, had practically whirled

To end their brief revisit to beds and tables
And go with Pike to see what lay to the west.
Lawless, these resolutes, no doubt, if left
To their own ways, but willing to sign up
For months of unyielding law and never a chance
To shrug it off for Saturday booze and whores,
Always in danger of somehow seeming to buck
This formal, narrow-nosed, broad-shouldered man
With the strong chin and almost womanly mouth
And, as the law set out, be tied to a pole
And scourged with a hundred strokes of an eight-strand whip,
Which is to say, eight hundred wounds, and add
To those the gouges of the many knots
Worked into the strands. So what? They volunteered,
Knowing, with Pike in charge, how it would be,
Cold, drawn out, starved beyond all thought or provision
And straying off the course as if this marksman,
Able to bring down grouse and running deer,
Lacked something when it came to aiming at landmarks.
Or was what he lacked any hint of will himself
To go where ordered if a chance arose
Of seeing some grand sight? And these rough men,
Uninfluenced by the books that helped keep him
Conscious of what discovery meant, of what
Had and had not yet been found, took in
The same deep shivering breaths as he to think
Of what might be, and how it would be to find it.
Now it began to look as if this trip
Might be the last for all sixteen. The Indians,
Pike said, "demanded ammunition, corn,
Blankets, kettles et cetera, all of which
They were refused." Outnumbered four to one
By warriors who pushed forward, quivering
To grab their knives and arrows and avenge
The flat denial, Pike's men took up arms

And backed off watchfully, still westward, till
The enemy stood glaring and did not follow.
All that tense way, Pike said, he felt ashamed
Because the Indians had grabbed from his troop a sword,
A tomahawk, an ax, and five canteens—
The first time, Pike said, "a savage took anything
From me, with the least appearance of force." The next day
The marchers reached the junction of the Arkansas
And Fountain Creek, which he understandably held
To be a branch of the Arkansas, no less.
Close to that junction, they joined logs in a breastwork,
Foreshadowing, if they had known, the fort
That later settlers built and lost their lives
Inside when Utes swooped down on early Pueblo.

His men secure against Pawnee afterthought,
Pike set out on the hike he must have planned
Since his eye first locked in the far-off peak
Ten days before. Now it was late November
In eighteen-six, a Monday. There was The Peak,
Just to the north, looking so close that Pike
And Miller, who had also gone along
With Pike on his slog toward the high point of a river,
With two more men blithely set out from camp
At one o'clock, "with an idea of arriving
At the foot of the mountain; but found ourselves obliged
To take up our nights lodging under a single
Cedar, which we found on the prairie, without
Water and extremely cold." Still not convinced
That a mountain could keep on backing off from them,
Pike and his men marched early that Tuesday morning
"With an expectation of ascending the mountain," but at night
Had to make camp—at, Pike declared, its base.
Wednesday: sure they would climb and descend by evening,
They left their blankets, everything, in camp.

They climbed, sometimes up almost vertical rocks,
Till evening, when they camped in a slit of a cave
On a steep slope. It had a slanting roof
Of reddish granite set with gray-green lichens;
A floor of turbulent rock. They had no blankets,
No food, only the water they got from snow,
Which lay waist-deep—either a better year
For snow than most are now, or Pike's report
Added some inches. Possibly the depth
Grew in proportion to his hunger and thirst
And to the "inequality of the rocks"
They had lain on. On that Thanksgiving morning
They crawled out groaning, stiff-limbed, with dry throats,
Shivering in the summer uniforms
Their leader's forethought had supplied them with
For the easy overnight climb he could clearly see,
Just up the way. But here's the thing that twists
The prism so Pike's dark blunders come through tinted:
He and his men stood on that wretched morning
To look the way they had come, and felt themselves
"Amply compensated" for their trials
"By the sublimity of the prospects below.
The unbounded prairie was overhung with clouds . . .
Like the ocean in a storm; wave piled on wave
And foaming, whilst the sky was perfectly clear
Where we were." Such was Pike, such were his men,
Feeding their starved cells on what they had seen
And hoped to see. They turned and went on up,
Steeply again, wasting their dwindling powers
Each time a foot slipped off a coated rock
Or plunged into a crack unseen in the snow,
Eyes on the high foothill Pike called "the summit
Of this chain." Soon they had a break: a long,
Flat ridge, red-soiled where subalpine wind
Had clawed away the protective scab of snow.

Then up again, pulling from rock to rock
By grabbing the branches of small limber pines,
Scaly and gray like tails of obliging lizards.
On top, out of breath, they saw once more the summit
Of "the Grand Peak, which was entirely bare
Of vegetation and covered with snow." For once,
Pike overestimated the distance left
To the mountain he had been so confident of climbing.
It was, he said, maybe sixteen miles away,
A day's march just to the base, "when I believe
No human being could have ascended to
Its pinical." Did he mean just in those
Conditions, hungry, miserably dressed,
And almost sure of yet more foodless days?
If he meant ever, that was one more time
His foresight was askew. Just fourteen years
From then, on a fine summer day, three men
Walked up, finding no sign that anyone
Had made it there before them. One thing's sure:
The peak Pike never knew would bear his name
Had conquered him. He called it Great or Grand,
When in fact, he might, in weariness and hunger,
Have written down Unconquerable Peak.
Pike stood like Moses on Mount Pisgah, looking
At land he'd never walk on. Then the clouds,
As if the Lord were saying "That's enough,"
Moved up and hid the top. Down from their summit
The party went, seeking out easier routes,
Two buffalo the next afternoon providing,
Finally, marrow and meat. On the fifth day
Of what set out to be an overnight trip
The party walked into camp where the rivers met.
And did Pike shake his head on arrival or allow
A rueful smile of defeat to twist his mouth,
Or make some grand speech to convey the heights

His party had seen? All he says is this:
"Arrived at our camp before night; found all well."
The next day, though it was snowing hard, the Pike impatience
"Would not permit my lying still at that camp."
He set out leading the fifteen westward again,
The Peak coming back in view when the snow had stopped
So Pike could mismeasure it and then go on,
Looking for greater wonders and always for sources—
Of the Red, which Pike like others thought was the same
As the Canadian, and of course not finding it,
And of the Arkansas, which he found, all right,
And then, he and his men having endured
Thin air and steep climbs in deep snow, ill-shod,
Four of the party losing toes to frostbite,
And Pike still able to note down, stiff fingered,
A "most sublime and beautiful" landscape,
Downstream, downslope they came upon a river
He thought, or claimed to think, was at last the Red
And therefore property of the U. S.,
But found it was the Rio Grande, and he
Trespassing on the king of Spain's possessions.
Under genteel arrest in New Spain for four months,
He smuggled out, with his men's help, reports
This time of use to his nation's forces. Later,
A general, young but respected, happy
In his career, he misread one more feature
Of his surroundings, when, having chased the British
Back from the Canadian shore where he had landed,
He sat to await a formal word of surrender.
Close by the place he chose was a magazine
The British had abandoned, and by design
Of the defeated general, or else
Just more Pike luck, the magazine blew up.
So Pike reached one more summit, one more source,
And this one not to be disputed. Dying,

He cried, "Push on, my brave fellows, and avenge
Your general." He had lived to thirty-four
And gone where, although for millennia
Others had been, surely none looked with eyes
Like his, triumphant over having reached
A goal not worth the striving as a means
To rations or defense but as a mark,
A source, a summit whose grand mystery
Made pain, to him, as level as the plains.

The quotations from Pike's journals, along with much of the biographical information, are taken from Donald Jackson's The Journals of Zebulon Montgomery Pike, with Letters and Related Documents (University of Oklahoma Press, 1966). Another source of biographical information was W. Eugene Hollon's The Lost Pathfinder: Zebulon Montgomery Pike (University of Oklahoma Press, 1949). Details of Pike's trek from the present site of Pueblo to the vicinity of Pikes Peak are drawn mainly from the persuasive research of John Patrick Michael Murphy.

German
Romantic Poets

Eduard Mörike

(1804-1875)

To the New Year

As, without sound
To us on the ground,
With feet all rose-hued,
An angel touched Earth,
So lowered the dawn.
You pious ones, shout
A loud welcome out,
A loud welcome out!
My heart, too, sound forth!

May all beginning
Be like His spinning
Of moons and of suns
Through Heaven's blue plain.
Thou, Father, give counsel!
Guide all on their way!
Lord, in thy hand may
All start and all stay,
All ever remain!

Zum neuen Jahr

Wie heimlicherweise
Ein Engelein leise
Mit rosigen Füßen
Die Erde betritt,
So nahte der Morgen.
Jauchzt ihm, ihr Frommen,
Ein heilig Willkommen,
Ein heilig Willkommen!
Herz, jauchze du mit!

In Ihm sei's begonnen,
Der Monde und Sonnen
An blauen Gezelten
Des Himmels bewegt.
Du, Vater, Du rate!
Lenke Du und wende!
Herr, Dir in die Hände
Sei Anfang und Ende,
Sei alles gelegt!

Love's Fortune

Since poets often, in warm fantasy
About love's bliss and its sombre delights
Mislead themselves or us in their wild flights,
Then for this jingle may they pardon me.

To me, though, God has given it graciously
To soar through their dream heaven day and night.
There, pleasure to my arm is nestled tight
And guiltless glances with quick fire burn free.

Love's pressing burdens I too used to bear,
Not scorning to take drafts from that harsh cup,
So that I might in fullness feel joy's beams.

And yet was like those poets' heady air,
My fortune without measure wafted up
So that I lose myself in waking dreams.

Liebesglück

Wenn Dichter oft in warmen Phantasieen,
Von Liebesglück und schmerzlichem Vergnügen,
Sich oder uns, nach ihrer Art, belügen,
So sei dies Spielwerk ihnen gern verziehen.

Mir aber hat ein gütger Gott verliehen,
Den Himmel, den sie träumen, zu durchfliegen,
Ich sah die Anmut mir im Arm sich schmiegen,
Der Unschuld Blick von raschem Feuer glühen.

Auch ich trug einst der Liebe Müh und Lasten,
Verschmähte nicht den herben Kelch zu trinken,
Damit ich seine Lust nun ganz empfinde.

Und dennoch gliech ich jenen Erzphantasten:
Mir will mein Glück so unermeßlich dünken,
Daß ich mir oft im wachen Traum verschwinde.

Too Much

The sky is glowing in pure springtime light,
The hill swells toward it, filled with love's deep yearning,
The stiff world melts away in blest love-turning
And all is poetry, sweet and aright.

In the steep village, by the wind-stirred spruce,
Is where my dear one's little house is laid--
Oh heart, what you have pondered and what weighed,
How could it all your battling joys reduce!

You, love, now sweep the sweet enchantment free
By which in all my being Nature storms!
And spring, bend love to yielding inclination!

Turn dark, oh day! Make night my remedy!
Since in you soft stars godly coolness forms,
I wish to enter the gulf of contemplation.

Zu Viel

Der Himmel glänzt vom reinsten Frühlingslichte,
Ihm schwillt der Hügel sehnsuchtsvoll entgegen,
Die starre Welt zerfließt in Liebessegen,
Und schmiegt sich rund zum zärtlichsten Gedichte.

Am Dorfeshang, dort bei der luftgen Fichte,
Ist meiner Liebsten kleines Haus gelegen--
O Herz, was hilft dein Wiegen und dein Wägen,
Daß all der Wonnestreit in dir sich schlichte!

Du, Liebe, hilf den süssen Zauber lösen,
Womit Natur in meinem Innern wühlet!
Und du, o Frühling, hilf die Liebe beugen!

Lisch aus, o Tag! Laß mich in Nacht genesen!
Indes ihr sanften Sterne göttlich kühlet,
Will ich zum Abgrund der Betrachtung steigen.

By the Woods

Long afternoons at woods' edge I have spent
Lying in grass, hearing the cuckoo call;
It seems to lull the vale in comfort, all
In peaceful unison with its lament.

There I am happy, and my constant pain,
The need to bear in calmness people's spite,
Here finally has ceased to be a fight
Where I find pleasure on my own again.

And if fine people could once see at last
How beautifully the poets waste their day,
They would feel envy of me in the end.

Because the sonnet's tight-strung wreaths can twist
Themselves as if my hand had had no say,
While toward the airy distance my eyes wend.

Am Walde

Am Waldsaum kann ich lange Nachmittage,
Dem Kukuk horchend, in dem Grase liegen;
Er scheint das Tal gemächlich einzuwiegen
Im friedevollen Gleichklang seiner Klage.

Da ist mir wohl, und meine schlimmste Plage,
Den Fratzen der Gesellschaft mich zu fügen,
Hier wird sie mich doch endlich nicht bekriegen,
Wo ich auf eigne Weise mich behage.

Und wenn die feinen Leute nur erst dächten,
Wie schön Poeten ihre Zeit verschwenden,
Sie würden mich zuletzt noch gar beneiden.

Denn des Sonetts gedrängte Kränze flechten
Sich wie von selber unter meinen Händen,
Indes die Augen in der Ferne weiden.

Johann Wolfgang von Goethe

(1749-1832)

The Harper

Who ne'er with tears has taken bread,
Who ne'er has spent the grim nights' hours
Sitting and weeping on his bed,
He knows you not, you heavenly powers.

You lead us till we life attain,
You let the wretch's guilt come forth,
Then you abandon him to pain,
Since all guilt is avenged on Earth.

Der Harfenspieler

Wer nie sein Brot mit Tränen ass,
Wer nie die kummervollen Nächte
Auf seinem Bette weinend sass,
Der kennt euch nicht, ihr himmlischen Mächte.

Ihr führt ins Leben uns hinein,
Ihr lasst den Armen schuldig werden,
Dann überlasst ihr ihn der Pein,
Denn alle Schuld rächt sich auf Erden.

The Finding-Again

Westöstlicher Divan VIII, 39

Can it be! Thou, star of clearness,
Once more to my heart held so!
Ah, the midnight of unnearness,
An abyss it is, a woe!
Yes, 'tis thou, O sweet, most cherished
Adversary of my joys!
Mindful of our grief, late perished,
I mistrust the present's poise.

When in deep primeval powers
Earth lay on his timeless heart,
God ordained the first of hours,
Joying in creation's art,
And his "Let there be!" resounded.
Then burst forth the darkest groan,
And the All with might unbounded
In reality was flown.

Light appeared on the horizon;
Darkness shyly left him so.
Elements, now, loose their ties on
Each the next, and quickly go.
Futilely and wildly dreaming,
Each one rushed to be apart,
Fixed, in boundless spaces' gleaming,
Having neither voice nor heart.

Hushed and barren was creation;
Lonely, for the first time, God.
Then he made dawn; from her station,

She, in pity, far abroad
For the suffering and the troubled
Hung her singing hues arrayed,
And again came love, redoubled,
To what, each from each, had fled.

And with hasty, zealous striving
Each seeks for itself its own,
Form and consciousness reviving
In their lives' once boundless zone.
Rashly or in moderation
Joined, let them grasp and cling.
Allah, rest from all creation—
Ours, now, be earth's fashioning.

Thus, on morning's new-red pinions,
To your lips was I propelled,
And night stamps the best of unions,
Firmly, thousandfold gold-sealed.
We alike on earth are meted
A surpassing joy and pain,
And no "Let there be," repeated,
Shall disjoin us again.

Wiederfinden

Westöstlicher Divan VIII, 39

Ist es möglich! Stern der Sterne,
Drück ich wieder dich ans Herz!
Ach, was ist die Nacht der Ferne
Für ein Abgrund, für ein Schmerz!
Ja, du bist es, meiner Freuden
Süsser, lieber Widerpart!
Eingedenk vergangner Leiden,
Schaudr' ich vor der Gegenwart.

Als die Welt im tiefsten Grunde
Lag an Gottes ew'ger Brust,
Ordnet' er die erste Stunde
Mit erhabner Schöpfungslust.
Und er sprach das Wort: "Es werde!"
Da erklang ein schmerzlich Ach,
Als das All mit Machtgebärde
In die Wirklichkeiten brach!

Auf that sich das Licht; so trennte
Scheu sich Finsternis von ihm,
Und sogleich die Elemente
Scheidend auseinander fliehn.
Rasch in wilden, wüsten Träumen
Jedes nach der Weite rang,
Starr, in ungemessne Räumen,
Ohne Sehnsucht, ohne Klang.

Stumm war alles, still und öde,
Einsam Gott zum erstenmal!
Da erschuf er Morgenröte,

Die erbarmte sich der Qual;
Sie entwickelte dem Trüben
Ein erklingend Farbenspiel,
Und nun konnte wieder lieben,
Was erst auseinander fiel.

Und mit eiligem Bestreben
Sucht sich, was sich angehört;
Und zu ungemessnem Leben
Ist Gefühl und Blick gekehrt.
Sei's Ergreifen, sei es Raffen,
Wenn es nur sich fasst und hält!
Allah braucht nicht mehr zu schaffen,
Wir erschaffen seine Welt.

So mit morgenroten Flügeln
Riss es mich an deinen Mund,
Und die Nacht mit tausend Siegeln
Kräftigt' sternenhell den Bund.
Beide sind wir auf der Erde
Musterhaft in Freud' und Qual,
Und ein zweites Wort: "Es werde!"
Trennt uns nicht zum zweitenmal.

The Violet

A violet stood in meadows green
With head downcast and all unseen.
It was a charming violet.
There came a youthful shepherd maid
With cheerful heart and lightsome tread
Across the fields with joy and song.

Ah! thinks the violet, if I were
The fairest bloom of all the fair
For just a tiny while yet!
So might I catch the dear one's eye
And in her bosom wilting lie
Ah, just a little moment long.

Ah! Well-a-day! she wandered there
And of her pathway took no care
But stepped upon the violet.
It sank and died, and yet was glad:
And so I die, yet am I dead
By her, beneath the dear one's tread.

Das Veilchen

Ein Veilchen auf der Wiese stand
Gebückt in sich und unbekannt;
Es war ein herzigs Veilchen.
Da kam eine junge Schäferin
Mit leichtem Schritt und munterm Sinn
Daher, die Wiese her und sang.
Ach, denkt das Veilchen, wär' ich nur
Die schönste Blume der Natur
Ach, nur ein kleines Weilchen.
Bis mich das Liebchen abgepflückt
Und an dem Busen matt gedrückt
Ach nur ein Viertelstündchen lang!

Ach! aber ach! das Mädchen kam
Und nicht in Acht das Veilchen nahm,
Ertrat das arme Veilchen.
Es sank und starb und freut' sich noch,
Und sterb' ich denn, so sterb' ich doch
Durch sie, zu ihren Füßen doch.

Wanderer's Night Song—I

You who come from heaven here,
Stilling all our grief and pain,
Him whose thoughts are doubly drear
Making doubly glad again,

I am tired of being rent.
Why can joy and pain not rest?
Sweet content,
Come, oh come into my breast.

Wandrers Nachtlied—I

Der du von dem Himmel bist,
Alles Leid und Schmerzen stillest,
Den, der doppelt elend ist,
Doppelt mit Erquickung füllest,

Ach, ich bin des Treibens müde!
Was soll all der Schmerz und Lust?
Süsser Friede,
Komm, ach komm in meine Brust!

Annette von Droste-Hülshoff

(1797-1848)

On the Tower

I stand on the balcony, high up a tower,
A starling screams in the air,
And like a maenad I yield to the power
Of storm fingers tousling my hair.

O fierce friend, so full of clownish rage,
I wish you were in my embrace
Where, sinew to sinew, two steps from the edge,
Our life-and-death fight could take place.

And down there so fresh, I see on the beach,
Like packs of loud hounds, wild and gay,
The waves hiss and hasten, rise, shatter, and breach,
Then crash up in glittering spray.

O, that I might plunge swiftly in,
Deep in the hounds' backs of foam,
And stalk through the forest of coral to win
The walrus, droll prey, to bring home.

Above me I see a pennant fly
Like a banner, a martial sight,
And see a boat whirled now low, now high
From this, my lofty lookout.

O if I could sit in that sea-pounded ship,
And tiller in hand, steer and pull
And over the rock reef skimmingly slip,
As light as a high-flying gull.

Were I a hunter and ranging free,
Or partly a soldier, perhaps,
Or a man, at least such minimally,
Then heaven would guide all my steps.

Here I must sit, though, all dainty and spruce,
Just like a well-brought-up child,
And only in private let my hair loose
To fly in the wind as if wild.

Am Turme

Ich steh auf hohem Balkone am Turm,
Umstrichen vom schreienden Stare
Und laß gleich einer Mänade den Sturm
Mir wühlen im flatternden Haare;

O wilder Geselle, o toller Fant,
Ich möchte dich kräftig umschlingen,
Und, Sehne an Sehne, zwei Schritte vom Rand
Auf Tod und Leben dann ringen!

Und drunten seh ich am Strand, so frisch
Wie spielende Doggen, die Wellen
Sich tummeln rings mit Geklaff und Gezisch,
Und glänzende Flocken schnellen.

O, springen möcht'ich hinein alsbald,
Recht in die tobende Meute,
Und jagen durch den korallenen Wald
Das Walroß, die lustige Beute!

Und drüben seh ich ein Wimpel wehn
So keck wie eine Standarte,
Seh auf und nieder den Kiel sich drehn
Von meiner luftigen Warte;

O, sitzen möcht ich im kämpfenden Schiff,
Das Steuerruder ergreifen,
Und zischend über das brandende Riff
Wie eine Seemöwe streifen.

Wär' ich ein Jäger auf freier Flur,
Ein Stück nur von einem Soldaten,
Wär'ich ein Mann doch mindestens nur,
So würde der Himmel mir raten;

Nun muß ich sitzen so fein und klar,
Gleich einem artigen Kinde,
Und darf nur heimlich lösen mein Haar,
Und lassen es flattern im Winde!

The Fish Pond

It lies as still in morning hours,
As peaceful, as a pious heart.
Its glass is kissed by west wind's art,
But untouched stand the shoreline flowers.
Above it tremble dragonflies,
Blue-gold and carmine, pencil-size,
And on the sunlight's mirrored glance
A water spider leads the dance.
An iris on the near bank grows
And hears the reeds' hushed slumber psalm;
A gentle riffling comes and goes,
As if it whispered: calm! calm! calm!

Der Weiher

Er liegt so still im Morgenlicht,
So friedlich, wie ein fromm Gewissen;
Wenn Weste seinen Spiegel küssen,
Des Ufers Blume fühlt es nicht;
Libellen zittern über ihn,
Blaugolde Stäbchen und Karmin,
Und auf des Sonnenbildes Glanz
Die Wasserspinne führt den Tanz;
Schwertlilienkranz am Ufer steht
Und horcht des Schilfes Schlummerliede;
Ein lindes Säuseln kommt und geht,
Als flüstre's: Friede! Friede! Friede!

To Philippa

Up in the East, the young light streams,
On waves its golden fragrance plays
And like a sweet face in my dreams
I see a distant, swelling sail.
Oh if but like a gull I might
Encircle it in joyful rings,
Oh, could I own the realm of air,
Own youthful and life-brightened wings!

Philippa, light around you streams.
You are encircled by dawn's breath,
You are a loved face seen in dreams
At my horizon's blurring death.
When your flag swells, so far off yet
And dreamlike ringed by fragrant dawn,
I wish somehow I might forget
Soon my horizons will be gone.

Forget, too, how my evening fell,
My light dimmed trembling, spark by spark,
My sail has long since ceased to swell,
My standard unseen in the dark.
Though those no more in youth extend,
Nor spread out freshly next to you,
Love, still, Philippa, I do send
And bless you all your voyage through.

An Philippa

Im Osten quillt das junge Licht,
Sein goldner Duft spielt auf den Wellen,
Und wie ein zartes Traumgesicht
Seh ich ein fernes Segel schwellen;
O, könnte ich der Möwe gleich
Umkreisen es in lustgen Ringen,
O, wäre mein der Lüfte Reich,
Mein junge, lebensfrische Schwingen!

Um dich, Philippa, spielt das Licht,
Dich hat der Morgenhauch umgeben,
Du bist ein liebes Traumgesicht
Am Horizont von meinem Leben;
Seh deine Flagge ich so fern
Und träumerisch von Duft umflossen,
Vergessen möcht ich dann so gern,
Daß sich mein Horizont geschlossen;

Vergessen, daß mein Abend kam,
Mein Licht verzittert Funk an Funken,
Daß Zeit mir längst die Flagge nahm
Und meine Segel längst gesunken;
Doch können sie nicht jugendlich
Und Frisch sich neben deinen breiten,
Philippa, lieben kann ich dich
Und segnend deine Fahrt geleiten.

The Word

Much like an arrow is a word,
And once, in jest or not, let go,
Swift in its passage from your bow,
Its haste may see your terror stirred.

Or it is like, out of your hand
Escaped, a seed, to who knows where?
And yet it thrives in soil there
And pushes roots down through the land.

Like a strayed sparklet, lost and free,
Perhaps quenched on a rainy day,
Or lighting up some leafy way
Or touching off some flaming sea.

And yet words can be dark and deep,
Can drop with such a weighty fall:
None is the emptiest of all,
For each you hope, or else you weep.

Oh, just from heaven's field one ray,
My God, to one afraid and blind!
How can he goals and harvest find?
How measure air or dewy spray?

Almighty one, who sent The Word
But kept from us what it will be,
Grant that your own gift may rule free,
By your will breathed to us, and heard!

Instruct the arrow how to go,
Nourish the sleep-drunk seedling well,
The straying spark quench or impel
For what it means, you only know.

Das Wort

Das Wort gleicht dem beschwingten Pfeil,
Und ist es einmal deinem Bogen
In Tändeln oder Ernst entflogen,
Erschrecken muß dich seine Eil.

Dem Körnlein gleicht es, deiner Hand
Entschlüpft; wer mag es wiederfinden?
Und dennoch wucherts in den Gründen
Und treibt die Wurzeln durch das Land.

Gleicht dem verlornen Funken, der
Vielleicht verlischt am feuchten Tage,
Vielleicht am milden glimmt im Hage,
Am dürren schwillt zum Flammenmeer.

Und Worte sind es doch, die einst
So schwer in deine Schale fallen:
Ist keins ein nichtiges von allen,
Um jedes hoffst du oder weinst.

O, einen Strahl der Himmelsau,
Mein Gott, dem Zagenden und Blinden!
Wie soll er Ziel und Acker finden?
Wie Lüfte messen und den Tau?

Allmächtger, der das Wort geschenkt,
Doch seine Zukunft uns verhalten,
Woll selber deiner Gabe walten,
Durch deinen Hauch sei sie gelenkt!

Richte den Pfeil dem Ziele zu,
Nähre das Körnlein schlummertrunken!
Erstick ihn oder fach den Funken!
Denn, was da frommt, das weißt nur du.

Friedrich Rückert

(1788 – 1866)

Dedication

You, all my soul and all my heart,
You, where all joys and sorrows start,
You, the whole world wherein I stay,
My heaven, in which I float away,
Oh you the grave I've often sought
Wherein my sorrows sink to naught.

You are my peace, you my repose,
You the best gift that heaven bestows.
That you love me makes me worthwhile,
My self I see best in your smile,
You, loving, lift me far on high,
My sweetest sprite, my better I.

Widmung

Du meine Seele, du mein Herz,
Du meine Wonn', o du mein Schmerz,
Du meine Welt, in der ich lebe,
Mein Himmel du, darein ich schwebe,
O du mein Grab, in das hinab
Ich ewig meinen Kummer gab.

Du bist die Ruh, du bist der Frieden,
Du bist vom Himmel mir beschieden.
Daß du mich liebst, macht mich mir wert,
Dein Blick hat mich vor mir verklärt,
Du hebst mich liebend über mich,
Mein guter Geist, mein beßres Ich!

The Fragrance of a Sweetgum Bough

The fragrance of a sweetgum bough
Sweetened the room,
A bough so pleasant,
A loving present
From a sweet whom.
How lovely was that sweetgum bough!
How lovely is that sweetgum bough!
The sweet gum branch,
Your gift's dear essence.
In this sweet scent,
This tender presence,
I breathe love's fragrance now.

Ich atmet' einen linden Duft

Ich atmet' einen linden Duft!
Im Zimmer stand
Ein Zweig der Linde,
Ein Angebinde
Von lieber Hand.
Wie lieblich war der Lindenduft!
Wie lieblich ist der Lindenduft!
Das Lindenreis
Brachst du gelinde;
Ich atme leis
Im Duft der Linde
Der Liebe linden Duft

From "Songs on the Deaths of Children"

The sun now will arise as bright
As if no ill had come by night.
The ill befell no one but me.
The sun shines universally.
You must not make night yours alone,
Sink it in light that has always shone.
Inside my tent a small lamp failed.
The world's eternal light be hailed!

Aus "Kindertotenlieder"

Nun will die Sonn' so hell aufgehn,
Als sei kein Unglück die Nacht geschehn!
Das Unglück geschah nur mir allein!
Die Sonne, sie scheinet allgemein!
Du mußt nicht die Nacht in dir verschränken,
Mußt sie ins ew'ge Licht versenken!
Ein Lämplein verlosch in meinem Zelt!
Heil sei dem Freudenlicht der Welt!

From "Songs on the Deaths of Children"

Now I see clearly why so dark a flame
You beamed to me at many and many an hour.
--Oh, eyes!—As if a single glance had power
To gather your whole strength in all that came.

No inkling had I, though, enwrapped in mist
Created by my sight-defeating doom,
The beam was set already to go home
To that place where all light beams first exist.

You wanted with your light to say to me:
It is you whom we wished we could stay near,
But fate has said to us, that cannot be.
Look at us now; soon we'll be far from here;

What as just eyes, these days, you seem to see,
In future nights as just stars will appear.

Aus "Kindertotenlieder"

Nun seh' ich wohl, warum so dunkle Flammen
Ihr sprühtet mir in manchem Augenblicke.
– O Augen! – Gleichsam, um voll in einem Blicke
Zu drängen eure ganze Macht zusammen.

Doch ahnt' ich nicht, weil Nebel mich umschwammen,
Gewoben vom verblendenden Geschicke,
Daß sich der Strahl bereits zur Heimkehr schicke,
Dorthin, von wannen alle Strahlen stammen.

Ihr wolltet mir mit eurem Leuchten sagen:
Wir möchten nah dir bleiben gerne!
Doch ist uns das vom Schicksal abgeschlagen.
Sieh' uns nur an, denn bald sind wir dir ferne!

Was dir nur Augen sind in diesen Tagen:
In künft'gen Nächten sind es dir nur Sterne.

The Broadest Mountain

Sierra Grande, New Mexico

Driving northwest across the antelope plains
You see it flitting across the highway, south,
North, south, where finally it stays, a hulk
And bare on top like the Sangre de Cristo,
Though just a captain to that four-star file,
Not half as high in feet above road level.
Its bareness and its broadness are its marks,
The bareness bearing grass and not real tundra,
Bare not from alpine cold that withers seedlings
But from the eastbound storms those westward caesars
Seize for themselves, so all the snow that clings
Here is a scab to scratch a mule deer's ankles,
Too little to sprout any tree that could survive
The mere subalpine chill on top. And broadness?
What does that have to do with mountains? Putting
Those nouns together is like saying a tenor
Has the best low tones of his kind. It's true,
The mountain fills a lot of sky, but only
Left-right, not up-down. On its lowest flanks
Grass grows, and plains weeds, plains flowers. Sliding up,
Your eye comes to the first trees, junipers
And piñons, dry-land darkeners, chest-high
To a mounted man but looking from the highway
Like shinnery to scuffle through while keeping
Watch for a rattlesnake. They do get taller
In their slow climb, and after, who knows, a mile,
Trees twice as tall rear up, the ponderosas,
Ragged and sparse but dominant. Up close,
They would have thick boles and warm red bark gemmed
With drops of rosin. On and on the eye goes,

Sideways much more than up. It's gradualness,
Taking its time, that makes this mountain broad.
A leisurely mountain, a lazy one. And gentle.
When pines, all trees, give up on finding height
Enough for wetness without too much cold,
The slopes, bare now, do not leap in new freedom
Like hikers who have just set down their packs,
But keep on lifting, easy, on both sides
Without competing to be first on top.
Top? It's too understated to be that,
Almost. The slopes meet there like table leaves,
Like mortised, friendly fingers, and if I
Had climbed, too, I doubt that my legs would know
For sure where to consider their work done,
All is so unassuming, so restrained.
A broad, slow rising mountain, and a low one,
But with a timberline of its own sort,
Not shown with tundra-brown on topo maps,
Not perilous with crags, needles, and cliffs,
But real, too high for any trees to grow
In cold and drouth. I claim kin to this mountain,
And, if my arms would stretch that many miles,
Would like to wrap its whole wide form up in them
And lay my cheek on its smooth top, and rest.

Wind

It seldom pauses, here, although it changes,
Rippling the buffalo grass green, rippling it brown,
Driving cloud shadows northeast, northwest, south
Across the pasture, filling the ditch with snow,
At the end of the field, that stays after the ground
Elsewhere is bare and swept or turning green.

Dents in the tall wheat, when fields are green,
Cross as if swished by dark hands feeling the changes
In texture, stem to moist head, and the windmill is ground
Ceaselessly, drawing clear water up from brown
Slushy sand, the return of many years' snow,
The under-us stream that parodies wind, inching south.

In June, when drying air moves in from the south,
The harvest calls all hands out, even the green
Boys, to parch long days in the wind, while the snow
Of whipped wheat dust clogs their eyes and throat, and the
changes
Of light to dark and back alike find the brown
Bare arms turning wheels, till the wind rasps in shaven ground.

Fall is when the wind backs off, leaving the ground
Unstirred sometimes for a day, but then from far south
Comes the skirt of the latest hurricane, reviving the brown
Heat-preserved grass with puissant air, calling the green
Back into stem and blade with wind that exchanges
Whips for caresses, damp forerunners of snow.

When that finally comes, it is rarely the calm snow

Of nostalgia, but screamingly comes and scours the hard ground,
Not stopping until a fence or a house rears and changes
Its impetus, glutting the north sides, sifting the south
Full of timed-release water, so later the green
Shows where we foiled the wind-driven purpose, the brown.

Though we live amid wind till it dries us wrinkled and brown
As the land it also shapes, and our hair turns to snow
Like John Anderson's, hope continues to green
In us self-deceivers, however feeble its ground,
That this restless monotony someday gives way, and the South
Sends its moist air that, heavy and still, never changes.

Even so, as wind pocks the snow, on the green-brown ground,
With brown, and fresh green snowbells brought from the South
Fall brown to that snow, and we weep for soft greens, nothing changes.

Shadow

Nobody notices it but me.
I can see it constantly.
Foggy or bright, outside or in,
Shorter or longer, it has just been—
Shorter when I was, suddenly long
When years began shrinking me. Right or wrong,
I live as its silent mother lamp:
Myself, a sedentary tramp.
I think my shadow will still be here
As long as I can make appear
A light the world will never see.
Though less than what was more of me
And dimmer, it yet serves to show
Myself out front wherever I go.

Acknowledgments

I am most grateful to Dagmar Grieder for her corrections and suggestions in my German Romantic translations, and to Loren Steffy, whose Stoney Creek Publishing made this book a reality as it had done with three earlier books of mine.

Previous Publications, with Thanks:

"The Need of More Navalnys," "A Modern Monster," and "Of Angels Bending Near the Earth,"

Oxford Magazine (UK)

"A Ghazal on the Threat of War," *National Review*

"From an Airplane at Night" and "Unbraced," *Nimrod International Journal*

"Approaching Herd," "The Return," "Defier of Gravity," "Mozart's Piano," and excerpts from

"Zebulon," *Pulsebeat* ("Defier of Gravity" later also in *Forgotten Ground Regained*)

"For My Granddaughters' Birthdays," V and VII, *The Lyric*

"Black Widow," "gnat," and "Praying Mantis," *Light*

"Moth" and "Cockroach," *Society of Classical Poets Journal*

"Fly," *Blue Unicorn*

"Cicada," *National Review*

"Cardinal," *Light*

"Changeable Presence" (earlier also in *Barrow Street*), " The Domestication," (earlier also in *JASAT—Journal of the American Studies Association of Texas*) "Sweet and Sour," "Low-Born Emperor," "Defier of Gravity" (earlier also in *Pulsebeat*), "Continuous Gestation," "Skyline Herds," "Change of Pace," "Ceaseless Laborer," and "Youth and Age," all in *Forgotten Ground Regained:A Journal of Alliterative Verse*

"The Finding-Again" (Goethe), *Measure*, 2013

"The Broadest Mountain," *Westview* and *Wolfe and Other Poems*, Wundor Editions, London

"Wind," *Iron Horse Literary Review* and *Wolfe and Other Poems*, Wundor Editions, London

About the Author

Donald Mace Williams is a retired newspaper writer and editor with a Ph.D. in Beowulfian prosody. His poems have appeared in five dozen magazines. *Wolfe*, his epic adaptation of *Beowulf*, set in the Old West, was released, along with his prose memoir, in *Wolfe and Being Ninety*. His poetry has also been collected in *The Nectar Dancer* and his translations of selected poems by Rainer Maria Rilke were released in 2025's *Poems of Rainer Maria Rilke: A 150th Anniversary Reader*. Williams is ninety-six and still writing. He lives in Austin, Texas.

www.ingramcontent.com/pod-product-compliance
Lightning Source LLC
LaVergne TN
LVHW091036270626
841918LV00001B/2
9781965766835